Art Profiles
For Kids

CLAUDE MONET

Mitchell Lane
PUBLISHERS

P.O. Box 196
Hockessin, Delaware 19707
Visit us on the web: www.mitchelllane.com
Comments? email us: mitchelllane@mitchelllane.com

ART PROFILES FOR KIDS

Titles in the Series

Antonio Canaletto

Claude Monet

Michelangelo

Paul Cézanne

Pierre-Auguste Renoir

Vincent van Gogh

Art Profiles
For Kids

CLAUDE MONET

Jim Whiting

Mitchell Lane
PUBLISHERS

P.O. Box 196
Hockessin, Delaware 19707
Visit us on the web: www.mitchelllane.com
Comments? email us: mitchelllane@mitchelllane.com

Copyright © 2008 by Mitchell Lane Publishers. All rights reserved. No part of this book may be reproduced without written permission from the publisher. Printed and bound in the United States of America.

Printing   2   3   4   5   6   7   8   9

Library of Congress Cataloging-in-Publication Data
Whiting, Jim, 1943–
    Claude Monet / by Jim Whiting.
        p. cm. — (Art profiles for kids)
    Includes bibliographical references and index.
    ISBN 978-1-58415-563-8 (library bound)
    1. Monet, Claude, 1840–1926—Juvenile literature. 2. Painters—France—Biography—Juvenile literature. 1. Monet, Claude, 1840–1926. II. Title.
ND553.M7W47 2007
759.4—dc22
                                                                                                2007000660

ABOUT THE AUTHOR: Jim Whiting has been a remarkably versatile and accomplished journalist, writer, editor, and photographer for more than 30 years. A voracious reader since early childhood, he has long been an admirer of Claude Monet and other Impressionist painters, and often attends exhibitions of their works. Mr. Whiting has written and edited about 250 nonfiction children's books. He lives in Washington State with his wife and two teenage sons.

ABOUT THE COVER: The images on the cover are paintings by the various artists in this series.

PHOTO CREDITS: p. 36—Roger Viollet/Getty Images; all other images are the works of Claude Monet.

                                                                                                PLB, PLB4

Table of Contents

Art Profiles for Kids

Claude Monet's *Impression: Sunrise* gave its name to Impressionism. Monet
dated the painting in 1872, but most art historians believe he created it the
following year. In 1985, the painting was stolen from the Musée Marmottan
in Paris. It was recovered five years later.

one

Impression: Sunrise
Makes a Big Impression

Claude Monet (pronounced moh-NAY) had a problem, and so did more than twenty other young French artists.

The time was the early 1870s. These artists were all trying to make a living from selling their paintings. It was a challenge for them because they painted in a different style from what was acceptable at the time. For years, their work had been largely dismissed, so hardly anyone would exhibit it. As a result, it was difficult for potential buyers to see their work.

At that time, the main way of selling art was at something called the Salon. This was an annual exhibition of paintings in Paris. Hundreds of painters wanted to show their works. There wasn't room for everyone, so a jury looked at all the paintings that had been submitted. It selected only some of them to be placed on display. The jury was very conservative. It operated under a set of artistic standards that had long been in place.

Monet and the others, including Camille Pissarro (pih-SAW-roh), Pierre-Auguste Renoir (ren-WAHR), and Alfred Sisley, were at the forefront of a different approach to painting. There was a lot of resistance to this new approach.

A few of these artists had actually had a few paintings accepted at the Salon in the past, but it wasn't where they wanted to keep showing their works. They decided to join together and put on their own exhibit. It was the first time that a group of artists had ever done something like that.

The exhibit opened in April 1874. It was in a large studio that belonged to a photographer named Gaspard-Félix Nadar. The artists called their exhibit Première Exposition de la Société Anonyme des Artistes, Peintres, Sculpteurs, Graveurs (First Exhibition of the Limited Society of Artists, Painters, Sculptors, Engravers).

The name may have sounded impressive, but the results were not. The opening day of the Société Anonyme exhibition attracted just 175 people. Closing day a month later was even worse, with only 54 people coming through. In contrast, thousands of art patrons thronged the Salon every day during its exhibition.

One reason for the low turnout might have been an especially harsh judgment made by an art critic named Louis Leroy. A week after the exhibition opened, he wrote an article for an arts magazine. The article was based on an imaginary conversation with a friend named M. (for Monsieur, or Mister) Vincent. Vincent had supposedly attended the Société Anonyme exhibition with Leroy. Vincent (who was actually speaking Leroy's opinions) didn't seem to like any of the paintings. He was especially harsh with Monet's works.

One of the works was called *Boulevard des Capucines*. To create this painting, Monet had gone into Nadar's studio a few weeks before the exhibit opened. He painted the same bustling street scene that people who were at the exhibit would see if they looked out the window.

"Vincent" didn't like *Boulevard des Capucines*. One of the reasons may have been the way in which people were portrayed. Previous artists often painted allusions from classical mythology to make their subjects seem heroic and especially grand. No detail was too small to be ignored.

The people that Monet depicted in *Boulevard des Capucines* weren't grand. In fact, they barely seemed to exist. Each person was depicted with just a few brushstrokes, and they all looked nearly the same. It was difficult to tell the people apart.

"Vincent" asked Leroy, "'Only, be so good as to tell me what those innumerable black tongue-lickings in the lower part of the picture represent?'

Artgoers were not prepared for *Boulevard des Capucines*, which depicted a late-winter street scene. None of the figures were recognizable. Some of the few spots of color are the pink dabs in the lower right corner, which probably are balloons.

"'Why, those are people walking along,' I replied.

"'Then do I look like that when I'm walking along the Boulevard des Capucines? Blood and thunder! So you're making fun of me at last?'

"'I assure you, M. Vincent . . .'

"'But those spots were obtained by the same method as that used to imitate marble: a bit here, a bit there, slap-dash, any old way. It's unheard-of, appalling! I'll get a stroke from it, for sure.'"[1]

"Vincent" had similar negative comments about nearly everything else he saw in the studio. Nothing seemed to please him, no matter who the artist was.

"A catastrophe seemed to me imminent, and it was reserved for M. Monet to contribute the last straw," Leroy continued.

"'Ah, there he is, there he is!' [Vincent] cried, in front of No. 98. 'I recognize him, papa Vincent's favorite! What does that canvas depict? Look at the catalogue.'

"'*Impression: Sunrise.*'"[2]

This painting depicts the harbor of the French seaport of Le Havre shortly after dawn. There is very little detail in the picture. Apart from an orange sun and some orange rays of sunshine, the entire painting is shown in shades of gray.

"'Impression—I was certain of it,'" says Vincent. "'I was just telling myself that, since I was impressed, there had to be some impression in it . . . and what freedom, what ease of workmanship! Wallpaper in its embryonic state is more finished than that seascape.' In vain I sought to revive his expiring reason . . . but the horrible fascinated him,"[3] Leroy concluded.

While the painters liked to think of themselves as "Independents," Leroy's derisive term—Impressionists—stuck. Soon the painters themselves took up the word, as though it were a badge of honor.

Leroy wasn't the only one to seize on the term *Impressionism*. Critic Emile Cardon wrote, "Dirty three-quarters of a canvas with black and white, rub the rest with yellow, dot it with red and blue blobs at random, and you will have an *impression* of spring before which the initiates will swoon in ecstasy.

"Smear a panel with grey, plonk some black and yellow lines across it, and the enlightened few, the visionaries, exclaim: Isn't that a perfect impression of the bois de Meudon?

"When the human figure is involved, it is another matter entirely: the aim is not to render its form, its relief, its expression—it is enough to give an impression with no definite line, no color, light or shadow; in the implementation of so extravagant a theory, artists fall into hopeless, grotesque confusion, happily without precedent in art, for it is quite simply the negation of the most elementary rules of drawing and painting. The scribblings of a child have a naivety, a sincerity which make one smile, but the excesses of this school sicken or disgust."[4]

Not everyone was so harsh. Before the exhibition had opened, an art critic named Armand Silvestre observed of the paintings, "A blond light pervades them, and everything is gaiety, clarity, spring festivals, golden evenings or apple trees in blossom. They are windows opening on the joyous countryside, on rivers full of pleasure boats stretching into the distance, on a sky which shines with light mists, on the outdoor life, panoramic and charming."[5]

Not long afterward, another critic expressed similar sentiments: "If their aims are to be described in a single word, we should need to coin the word Impressionists. They are Impressionists in that they do not reproduce a landscape but convey the impression it makes on the beholder."[6]

In all, the Impressionists would have seven more exhibitions, with the final one coming in 1886. The negative criticism continued almost until the end. Typical was a comment after the second exhibition in 1876. "Five or six lunatics blinded by ambition, one of them a woman, have put their work on show," said critic Albert Wolff. "These self-appointed artists call themselves rebels, Impressionists; they take a canvas, brush and paint, fling on the colors indiscriminately, and then sign the thing."[7]

Monet used his girlfriend Camille Doncieux as the model for *Woman in the Green Dress*, one of his early successes. She was nineteen at the time.

Despite all the negative comments, Impressionism would become one of the most popular forms of art in the world. This popularity has continued to the present day. Exhibits of Impressionist paintings in museums all over the world nearly always draw huge crowds.

One of the more popular artists represented at these exhibitions is still Claude Monet.

Traditional French Painting

Many scholars believe that classical French painting began with Nicolas Poussin, who lived between 1594 and 1665. At that time, Italian art—which was based on the antiquities of Rome—was the dominant influence in the art world. Poussin spent considerable time in Rome, then returned to his native France. In his view, art was important because it provided illustrations of the proper ways in which people should behave. He believed that art was not art unless it conveyed a moral value.

Reflecting the influence of Poussin, the Académie royale de peinture et de sculpture (Royal Academy of Painting and Sculpture) was established in Paris in 1648. It set forth a very rigid course of study. The primary themes dealt with history, mythology, scenes from the Bible, and portraits of famous and important people. The subjects that the Académie students painted reflected the same principles of the great masters who had preceded them.

The Académie royale de peinture et de sculpture merged with several other schools in 1816 to form the Académie des beaux-arts (Academy of Fine Arts), but not much changed. The emphasis was still on line over color, on using conservative colors, and on portraits and still lifes over landscapes. Sometimes the painters would go out into the field, but the main purpose of being outside was to make sketches of what they saw. Then they would return to their studios and create the finished product with their paints.

They believed in including as much detail as possible, so they were very painstaking in their work. They wanted everything to seem lifelike. They also believed that all evidence of brushstrokes should be eliminated. That way, the viewer's attention would be on the artwork rather than on the painter who had created it. The result was a smooth finish.

The Shepherds of Arcadia by Poussin

The aim of these artists, above all, was to exhibit their works in the annual Salon, which was sponsored by the Académie des beaux-arts. The exhibition rooms would be packed floor to ceiling with paintings. For years, the Salon represented the road to respectability for painters. Being shown there was necessary for commercial success.

View of Rouelles is the first painting Monet exhibited. Rouelles was a small village just outside of Le Havre. The work shows that Monet was already interested in the effects of light.

two

Early Life

Claude Monet was born in Paris on November 14, 1840. His father was Adolphe Monet, and his mother was Louise-Justine Monet. Claude joined an older brother named Léon.

Adolphe Monet was a grocer. It's likely that he wasn't very successful. In 1845 the family moved to the seaport city of Le Havre. Adolphe went into business with his brother-in-law Jacques Lecadre, a grocer and ship chandler. A ship chandler sells things ships require.

Little is known of Claude's early life. He probably began school when he was about ten. His classes—typical of the times—included French grammar, math, Latin, Greek, and other subjects. There are no records of his grades, which probably weren't too good. In fact, no one knows if he even managed to graduate.

As he recalled much later, "This childhood of mine, was essentially one of freedom. I was born undisciplineable. No one was ever able to make me stick to the rules, not even in my youngest days. It was at home that I learned most of what I do know. I equated my [school] life with that of a prison and I could never resolve to spend my time there, even for four hours a day when the sun was shining bright, the sea was so beautiful and it was so good to run along the cliff-tops in the fresh air or frolic in the sea."[1]

He took one subject seriously. This was drawing. His teacher, Jean-Francois Ochard, had some fame as a painter. Ochard also taught several other successful French artists.

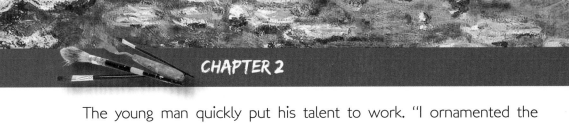
The young man quickly put his talent to work. "I ornamented the margins of my text books," he said. "I decorated the blue paper of my exercise books with ultra fantastic designs and represented in the most irreverent manner possible, the features of my masters—either drawing their faces in front view or in profile. I became very quickly adept at this game. At fifteen, I was known by the whole of Le Havre as a caricaturist."[2]

A caricaturist exaggerates some of the subject's facial features. For example, the subject may have a prominent nose. The caricaturist makes the nose even larger so that it becomes the dominant feature in the picture. Yet the subject must still be recognizable. The humor lies on contrasting the subject's real appearance with how he or she is portrayed.

Monet continued, "My reputation was so well established that I was commissioned by everyone for these types of portraits. It was in effect, in consideration of the sheer number of commissions that I received as well as the insufficiency of the allowance that I received from my mother, that prompted the audacious decision that I made to charge a fee for my portraits. This of course, scandalized my family. I would charge ten to twenty francs depending on whether I liked the look of my clients or not and this method worked extremely well. In a month, the number of clients had doubled and I was able to charge a fixed rate of twenty francs without reducing in any way the demand. Had I continued this way, I would today be a millionaire!

"Thus, by this means, I became someone of importance in the town. There, along the shop front of the only framers in business at Le Havre, were my caricatures, insolently sprawled-out in groups of five or six, to be seen in full in little gold frames, under glass like real works of art. Moreover, when I saw strollers gathering to gape at them with admiration and cry 'It is so and so!' I was bursting with pride."[3]

His caricatures shared space in the framing shop with landscapes and maritime scenes by a painter named Eugène Boudin. Monet didn't think much of Boudin. In that era, landscape artists would make some preliminary sketches outside, then do most of the actual painting in their indoor

Caricatures by Monet. A caricaturist may dramatically enlarge the size of the subject's head. It will then be placed on a relatively tiny body.

studios. Boudin had no studio. He did all his work in the outdoors. He said, "Everything that is painted directly and on the spot always has a force, a power, a vivacity of touch that cannot be re-created in a studio."[4]

Monet scoffed at this viewpoint. "[Boudin's] paintings inspired me with a terrible aversion and without even having met the man, I disliked him intensely,"[5] he said.

The framer urged Monet to meet Boudin. He explained that Boudin had studied at a well-known art school in Paris. Perhaps the youngster could learn something from the older man. Monet shook his head. He doubted that Boudin had anything to offer him.

One day, probably sometime in 1857, Monet happened to walk into the framing shop while Boudin was there. The framer introduced them.

According to Monet, Boudin said, "I always look at your sketches with pleasure; they are amusing, animated, they seem to have been done with ease. You have talent, one can see that straight away. But you are not, I hope, going to keep doing the same thing. It is very good for starting off, but you will get bored with just doing caricatures. Study, learn to look, paint and draw. Do some landscapes. It is so beautiful the sea and sky, animals, people and trees just as nature made them, with their characters, their true essence of being, in the light, within the atmosphere, just as things are."[6]

On this and several other occasions Boudin even offered to give Monet free lessons in painting outdoors. Though he found that he liked Boudin as a person, Monet always managed to find some excuse to decline.

Finally Boudin's persistence paid off. "I had no feasible excuse left to give him and gave in," Monet continued. "Thus it was, that Boudin—with his inexhaustible kindness—took it upon himself to educate me. With time, my eyes began to open and I really started to understand nature. I also learned to love it. I would analyze its forms with my pencil. I would study its colorations."[7]

He continued, "Suddenly a veil was torn away. I had understood—I had realized what painting could be. By the single example of this painter devoted to his art with such independence, my destiny as a painter opened out to me."[8]

In those days, becoming a painter in France meant one thing: going to Paris, the unquestioned cultural capital of Europe. His mother might have supported him in this newfound desire, but she died in 1858.

Adolphe Monet was much less sympathetic to his son's wish to choose painting as a career. He wanted Claude to follow in his footsteps in the grocery business. It was prospering and provided a secure, steady income. Painters, on the other hand, usually had to struggle to make a living. Monet thought he didn't need his father's financial support. He had saved much of the money from his caricatures and believed he could provide for himself.

"Armed with references acquired through admirers of Boudin," Monet said, "I promptly left for Paris without a care in the world."[9]

While Monet later claimed that he departed for Paris at the age of sixteen, that probably isn't accurate. In 1858, when he was seventeen, he exhibited his first known painting—*View of Rouelles*—in Le Havre. That meant he was still living in the city where he had grown up.

It's likely that his first trip to Paris occurred the following year, when he was eighteen. He enrolled in the Académie Suisse, an art studio, where he met Camille Pissarro. Pissarro would later become one of the founders of Impressionism.

In 1860 Monet was drafted into the French army. At that time it was possible to buy off one's military obligation. Apparently Monet's father wanted to do that—but he attached a string. His son would have to return to Le Havre, give up his dream of being an artist, and take his place in the family grocery business. Monet turned him down. He also thought that being a military man would be fun.

"The seven years which to many others seemed so difficult, appeared to me to be full of charm," he recalled. "A friend who loved military life, had communicated to me his enthusiasm and suffused me with his sense of adventure. Nothing seemed more attractive than the endless trekking under the sun, the raids, the crackle of the gun-powder, the sabre-rattling, the nights spent under canvas in the desert and I imperiously waved aside all my father's objections. I was 'bad news' and I obtained, on demand, that I should be sent to a regiment in Africa and left.

"I spent two really charming years in Algeria. There was always something new to see and in my spare time, I tried to capture what I saw. You cannot imagine the extent of what I learned and how much my ability to see improved. I was not immediately aware of this. The impressions of light and color that I gained there were, to some extent, put aside later, but the kernel of my future researches came from them."[10]

Monet's period of service ended abruptly when he acquired a serious case of typhoid fever and had to come home to recuperate. He spent six months recuperating at home, and during that time he met a Dutch painter named Johan Jongkind. Jongkind, who painted sun-drenched landscapes, became a great influence on the young man.

"He asked to see my sketches, invited me to come and work with him, explained the whys and wherefores underlining his work and thereby, completed the training that I had already received from Boudin," Monet recalled. "He became from this moment, my true master and it is to him, that I owe the definitive training of my eyes."[11]

When Monet had recovered, he was expected to return to his army unit. This time, his aunt was able to buy him out. He still wanted to go to Paris and become a painter. His aunt agreed, but attached one condition: Monet had to study with a man named Charles Gleyre.

Gleyre was a traditional painter, yet he allowed his students to experiment. His studio had one other advantage. It was there that Monet met three other students his age: Sisley, Renoir, and Frédéric Bazille. The young artists became good friends and important influences on one another.

It wasn't an easy life. Monet and Renoir lived together for a while, pooling what little money they could earn from commissions and portraits. Once they lived for an entire month on a sack of beans. Living in poverty hardly mattered. Renoir later said it was the happiest period of his life.

It was also a period of ferment in painting and other arts. In 1863, French leaders had established the Salon des Refusés (ray-fyoo-SAY), an exhibition of paintings rejected by the Salon. The purpose was to show that Salon judges were correct in their assessment. Nearly all the works in the exhibit were so bad that people who attended laughed at them.

However, one painting in the Salon des Refusés created a sensation. It was *Dejeuner sur l'Herbe*, or *Luncheon on the Grass*. The artist, Édouard Manet, featured two well-dressed young men and two women having a picnic. One of the women is nude.

Other painters had depicted nude women before, but they were classical subjects taken from mythology, history, or the Bible. Manet was the first to paint an everyday woman in the nude. Suddenly Manet became a primary focus of the young artists who wanted to rebel against the Salon and its restrictive, conventional standards.

Gustave Courbet became another icon for the movement. "Courbet insisted that only the actual, tangible objects which existed in a real world, without imaginative embellishment, idealization or alteration in the presentation of any subject, were acceptable,"[12] notes art historian Trewin Copplestone.

Yet it still was a fact of life that painters seeking to be recognized needed to exhibit at the Salon. Monet knew that trying to enter prematurely would do him more harm than good. In 1865, he thought he was ready.

Édouard Manet

Manet's *Self-Portrait with a Palette*

Édouard Manet was born in Paris on January 23, 1832. His mother was distantly related to the king of Sweden, and his father was a judge. Not surprisingly, Édouard's father wanted him to have a career in the law, but from an early age, the young man was interested in the arts. His uncle encouraged him in this ambition and frequently took him to the Louvre art museum.

His desire to become an artist received a boost when he failed the examination to join the French navy at the age of eighteen. For six years he studied under the academic painter Thomas Couture. He also traveled widely, which allowed him to see the works of many famous traditional painters.

Manet soon broke with this tradition. He was more interested in showing people in their normal lives and in landscapes than in history and mythology. He became notorious in 1863 with *Déjeuner sur l'Herbe* (*Luncheon on the Grass*) because of his use of nude models. His 1863 *Olympia* was no less scandalous. He updated a noted painting called *Venus of Urbino* by the famous classical painter Titian. Titian's painting also features a nude, but she is a goddess and shows a modest demeanor. That was acceptable. Manet's *Olympia* was actually a prostitute who glared defiantly outward. That was definitely not acceptable.

He became friendly with Impressionists, and his images of people enjoying themselves in contemporary society reflected the same interests as the Impressionists'. He created many enduring images of everyday life in Paris.

But Manet always believed that genuine success came from showing at the Salon. He refused to take part in the separate exhibitions of the Impressionists. He also used large blocks of black in his works, which the Impressionists never did. While he sometimes painted outdoors as they did, he regarded his studio work as more important.

According to art historian Lisa MacDonald, "Always controversial, Manet sought to record the days of his life using his own unique vision. From beggars, to prostitutes, to the bourgeoisie he sought to be true to himself and to reproduce 'not great art, but sincere art.'"[13]

He became very ill in the early 1880s and died on April 30, 1883.

The sun-drenched garden that Monet portrayed in *Women in the Garden* reflected his own happiness. His family was proud of his recent success in having some paintings accepted for the Salon and offered him financial support. Within a few months, however, they withdrew this support. Monet became desperate for money. A friend purchased this painting, which helped him to survive.

three

Years of Struggle

To Monet's surprise and delight, two of the paintings he submitted to the Salon in 1865 were selected for exhibition. Both of them were beach and sea scenes that he painted near Le Havre. One critic even said, "The two marines of M. Monet are unquestionably the best in the exhibition."[1]

At about this time, Monet met Camille Doncieux. Seven years younger than he was, she immediately became his model. That meant she posed for his paintings. They also began a love affair.

Monet was the kind of man who loved to compete. He wanted to paint something similar to Manet's work, but more impressive. To make sure that everyone got the point, he gave his new work the same title as Manet's: *Déjeuner sur l'Herbe*. It was a huge canvas, measuring thirteen feet by twenty feet. All dozen or so figures were life-sized. There were no naked women; everyone was stylishly dressed. Camille was the model for most of the women. Bazille obligingly posed for four of the six male characters. Monet painted a smaller version in the open air, then went into his studio and tried to complete the much larger work.

The project proved to be much too ambitious for Monet, and he couldn't complete it in time for the 1866 Salon. However, fragments and several studies still exist.

Still hoping to meet the Salon deadline, he painted Camille in a work entitled *Woman in a Green Dress*. According to legend, he needed only four days to complete it. The painting was accepted by the Salon and created a sensation. Critics were especially impressed by the manner in which Monet depicted the green silk dress Camille was wearing.

Spurred by this success, he embarked on another large figure study. In spite of the Salon's response to his Le Havre seascapes, there was a general belief that portraits were much more acceptable than seascapes or landscapes. Called *Women in the Garden*, this new work was about seven feet high and five feet wide. It showed four women, and Camille was the model for each one. When Monet painted it outdoors, he had to lower his easel into a trench in the ground in order to reach the top.

In terms of the artist's development, the painting is especially remarkable for its study of light. The sunlight on the ground that runs from one side of the picture to the other seems almost like a bright carpet. Monet showed the effects of light on each of the four figures. The work was also among his first depictions of gardens. The garden theme would become increasingly important to him, both as a person and as a painter.

However, *Women in the Garden* was turned down for the 1867 Salon. The people who ran the Salon were becoming concerned with Monet's increasing reputation. He painted in a style different from what was generally acceptable. They decided they wouldn't encourage him anymore.

That wasn't Monet's only problem. In spite of his Salon successes, he wasn't making much money from his artwork.

In addition, his father and the rest of his family strongly disapproved of his relationship with Camille. Their distaste became even stronger when she became pregnant, and they cut off the small allowance they had been providing him.

Things were so bad that Monet had to pretend he had broken off his relationship with Camille. His family then welcomed him back home. Camille gave birth to their son Jean in Paris on her own in 1867, while Monet remained in Le Havre.

Soon he was reunited with his girlfriend and new son, but he still had very little money. He began begging for money from his fellow artists and other friends. Bazille was especially generous. He bought *Women in the Garden* for a large sum of money, but it wasn't enough. Monet became especially discouraged, since his paintings for the Salon were continually rejected. He even claimed that he tried to commit suicide by throwing himself into the Seine River. No one knows for sure. He might have said that in order to improve his chances of getting money when he begged.

In the fall of 1868, Monet received a commission from a man named Louis-Joachim Gaudibert for a portrait of his wife and some other works. That provided him with just enough money to get by.

He was living not far from his relatives, though they refused to see Camille or the new baby. In December 1868 he wrote to Bazille: "Here I am surrounded by the things I love. I spend my time in the open, on the beach in stormy weather or when the fishing boats put out. . . . In the evenings, my dear friend, there is a warm fire in my cottage, and the cosiness of a small family. . . . Thanks to the help of [Gaudibert], I am now enjoying a spell of quiet, free of chores. Ideally I should like to stay in a peaceful nook like this forever."[2]

"Forever" ended within a very short time. His creditors forced him to leave the coast and flee to Paris. They seized many of his paintings.

Back in Paris, Monet continued to work on his style. His canvases increasingly reflected the play of light on various surfaces. His brush-strokes became short and choppy.

Monet finally married Camille in the summer of 1870. Soon afterward, the Franco-Prussian War broke out. Monet briefly left Camille and Jean behind as he quickly fled to England. As a former soldier, he was afraid that he would be called up for military service. The eager adventurer of less than a decade before had ceased to exist.

Monet's judgment in running away may have proved wise. His friend, fellow painter, and dedicated supporter Frédéric Bazille chose to become a soldier. He was killed shortly after the outbreak of the fighting.

Monet's wife and son soon joined him in London. They remained there for nearly a year and a half. Monet was especially fascinated by the frequent fogs that swirled around the city. He painted many pictures that captured the mysterious mood of bridges and buildings rising out of the mist. One of the most important things that happened to Monet during this time was meeting art dealer Paul Durand-Ruel. Durand-Ruel would play a crucial role in the artist's future success. A few months after the war ended in 1871, Monet came back to France.

He, Camille, and Jean settled in the village of Argenteuil, located on the banks of the Seine River a few miles outside of Paris. The family appeared to be free of money worries. Monet was selling some of his paintings, Camille had received a small dowry from her family when she married, and Monet's father had died, leaving him with a modest inheritance. They were able to afford two servants and a gardener.

Monet continued his interest in gardening. The garden at his house was the scene of numerous pictures, many of which featured Camille and Jean. Monet could also afford a small boat, which he converted into a portable studio. It allowed him to go out on the water and increased the number of possibilities for his painting. Over the next couple of years, he created several masterpieces depicting sailboats on the water with modern bridges in the background.

It was during this time that the first exhibition of the Société Anonyme was held. It didn't have much of an impact on sales of what were now being called Impressionist paintings.

That was perhaps one reason why he wrote Manet late in 1875: "Things are going worse and worse. Since the day before yesterday I have not had a sou, and no credit anywhere either—not at the butcher's, not at the baker's. Even if I have confidence in the future, the present remains very difficult. Could you send me 20 francs by return? It would tide me over for the moment."[3]

Yet as art historian Paul Hayes Tucker points out, Monet was apparently more prosperous than he was willing to admit. "During the course of his seven years at Argenteuil, he averaged more than 14,000 francs a year [more than the average physician and lawyer in Paris], which dispels all myths about his constant so-called proverty," Tucker writes. "Although he would continue to claim he was penniless and beg friends for spare change, he clearly was not destitute. He simply lived the good life and too often spent more than he had."[4]

By this time, Monet's desire to remain in Argenteuil was lessening. The village had become increasingly industrialized. Its location not far downstream from Paris also worked against it.

Starting in the 1850s, a man named Baron Georges-Eugène Haussmann had made radical changes to the design of the city of Paris. Its sparkling new vistas had provided inspiration for many painters, including Monet himself in the 1860s.

Unfortunately, according to Haussmann's design, most of the sewage from Paris drained into the Seine River and was carried downstream to Argenteuil. In 1878 Monet decided to look for another place to live. He soon found it in the village of Vétheuil.

That led to a highly unusual living arrangement. Several years earlier, a wealthy man named Ernest Hoschedé had begun purchasing some of Monet's paintings. Monet had even spent time at Hoschedé's country mansion, painting panels for one of the walls. Unfortunately Hoschedé's financial position came crumbling down in a very short period of time. He had to sell his paintings and give up his mansion and apartment in Paris.

Monet invited Hoschedé to come live with him and his family in Vétheuil. Hoschedé brought along his wife, Alice, and their five children. Alice soon gave birth to a sixth child.

By that time, Ernest Hoschedé had abandoned his family and fled to Belgium. Alice and her six children remained with Monet.

Then personal tragedy struck. Camille had given birth to a second child, Michel, in the spring of 1878. She was never in good health after that and died on September 5, 1879. She was only thirty-two. Alice had helped take care of her during her long illness.

No one is sure of the exact nature of the relationship between Alice and Monet before Camille's death. Afterward they lived virtually as man and wife, but they weren't legally married.

As a widower, Monet was in a position to remarry. Almost certainly he wanted to. The problem was Alice's situation. It must have seemed apparent to Alice that her husband would never return. He often sent letters to her, threatening to commit suicide because of his financial

Monet painted *Portrait of Jean Monet* in 1880, when Jean was twelve or thirteen.

troubles. Yet even if Alice had wanted to get a divorce, she couldn't. She was a practicing Catholic, and at that time the Catholic Church refused to allow divorce. The odd living arrangement (Monet, Alice, and their combined eight children) continued. There seems to be little doubt that Monet was very fond of Alice's children, and Alice in turn liked Jean and Michel.

As the children grew older, Monet and Alice wanted to give them better schooling than Vétheuil could offer. They thought they had found an ideal location, in the Paris suburb of Poissy, and moved there late in 1881. The schools may have been better, but for Monet, the working conditions were not. In spite of leaving town on several occasions for extended painting trips while Alice cared for the children, he wasn't satisfied with living there.

Less than two years later, Monet found a small farm just outside a village named Giverny. He had no way of knowing it, but his days of wandering were over. Monet would live almost exactly half his life in this one spot.

Modernizing Paris

Until well into the nineteenth century, the city of Paris reflected its medieval origins. The streets were narrow and winding, and it was difficult to get around. People were crammed together in tiny, centuries-old apartments. Garbage piled up in the streets.

In 1838 a French nobleman wrote, "How ugly Paris seems after a year's absence. How one chokes in these dark, narrow and dank corridors that we like to call the streets of Paris! One would think that one was in a subterranean city, that's how heavy is the atmosphere, how profound is the darkness!"[5]

With the French economy becoming stable in the 1840s and 1850s, many more people were becoming well-off. They wanted to make it easy to get around the city. They wanted good housing. They also wanted parks where they could relax and enjoy themselves, and treelined boulevards where they could go for a stroll.

In 1853 the French emperor, Napoleon III, addressed these problems. He ordered the prefect, or mayor, of Paris, Baron Georges-Eugène Haussmann, to undertake a massive program of civic improvements.

Haussmann rolled up his sleeves and went to work. He ordered thousands of workers to demolish dilapidated apartment buildings and rip up the narrow, confining streets. Newer and more elegant buildings rose alongside wide, treelined boulevards. He also built huge public parks such as the Bois de Boulogne.

To many people, these changes made Haussmann a hero. Paris became much cleaner, much lighter, and it was far easier to get around the city.

To others, however, he was a villain. Thousands of people were displaced when

Manet's *Racecourse in the Bois de Boulogne*

the apartments they lived in were destroyed. For well over a decade, there was constant noise and confusion as the changes were made. There were suggestions that the changes made the city less intimate. People didn't get to know one another as well as they had before.

The project was also very expensive. Napoleon and Haussmann eventually disagreed with each other. Napoleon fired him in 1870.

The city still reflects Haussmann's influence. Most people agree that it is one of the loveliest cities in the world.

Monet painted this self-portrait in 1886, the year of the final
Impressionist group exhibition. The Impressionists were already
going in new, separate directions. Monet did not participate in
the exhibit.

Giverny

Somewhat on an impulse, Monet signed a lease on the farm in Giverny right away. He didn't have enough money in his pocket to afford it. Fortunately Durand-Ruel—who was beginning to sell Monet's paintings more regularly—loaned him enough money to pay for moving expenses and a few months' rent.

Monet soon found that living at Giverny presented an awkward situation. Many of his neighbors were farmers who didn't approve of Monet's vocation as a painter. They also disapproved of the living arrangements. They knew that Alice and Monet weren't married.

Monet's neighbors weren't afraid of showing their disapproval. Sometimes they would cut down trees that Monet was trying to paint. Often they would charge him money for crossing their property.

For Monet, at least, there was the chance to get away from Giverny and go on lengthy trips. He frequently returned to the rugged coastline around Le Havre. Once he was nearly drowned when a freak wave washed over him.

With his friend and fellow painter Renoir, he also made a trip to the Mediterranean coast of France. He enjoyed it so much that he made several return trips on his own. Some of his most memorable paintings depict the scenery he found there.

These absences weren't always popular with Alice. When Monet was gone, she had to take care of all eight children by herself. Not surprisingly, that created a certain amount of discord in their relationship.

On the other hand, when Monet was home, he was able to indulge his passion for gardening. He and Alice planted many flowers and other types of foliage. The house and grounds quickly became a refuge for the family. No matter what their neighbors thought of them, they had each other and the pleasure of continually improving their surroundings.

Monet later claimed that he hadn't done anything special with his garden. He said that he had simply looked through gardening catalogs and ordered haphazardly. But the garden reflected a great deal of knowledge about plants and many hours of forethought and actual work. Monet and Alice didn't do all the work themselves. The garden eventually grew so large that it required the services of six full-time gardeners.

The efforts paid off. As a visitor noted, "Wherever one turns, at one's feet or head or at chest height there are pools, chains of flowers, blossoming hedges at once wild and cultivated, changing with the seasons, ever becoming new."[1]

As the garden developed, Monet began using it more and more as a site for his painting. One time he wanted to paint a large oak tree without any leaves. Overnight it began to bud, but Monet didn't want to start over. He paid several of the village children to climb the tree and remove every trace of green. That way he was able to complete the painting in the way that he had originally envisioned.

The year 1886 was especially important. The Impressionists held their eighth and final group exhibition. By then the group had become splintered. They were all strong-minded individuals with differing ideas about art. Monet chose not to exhibit anything in this final exhibition.

One reason was that his days of watching every penny had come to an end, largely because of Durand-Ruel. In the 1880s he opened an office in New York City. America was rapidly growing as an industrial power, and people were getting rich as the country's economy continued to boom. Many chose to spend their money on art, and they especially loved the Impressionists. Durand-Ruel was able to do a brisk business in New York for Monet and his fellow painters.

Monet's house and garden had subsequently become somewhat of a magnet to other painters, especially young artists from the United States. They set up their own studios in Giverny near Monet's home.

By 1890 Monet had earned enough money—much of it coming from the United States—to finally buy his house at Giverny. The next year Ernest Hoschedé died. His death allowed Alice to marry Monet. Their wedding took place on July 16, 1892.

By this time Monet's work habits were well established. He became very irritable if they were disrupted in any way.

He would wake up early, usually about four or five in the morning. He'd immediately look out his bedroom window to see what the weather was like. If he liked what he saw, he would take a cold bath and then eat a large breakfast. Then he would set out to paint. Often family members accompanied him. They would carry his equipment.

He would return for lunch, which had to be served precisely at 11:30. After eating and a brief rest, he would go back outside and resume his work. Sometimes he might also work in his studio.

At 7:00 he would eat dinner. While he didn't prepare the meals himself, he liked to eat well and there are several books of the recipes that he developed. He liked to share dinner with other people, and he didn't have to worry about finding company. By this time he was so famous that he had many visitors, including the numerous painters who had set up their studios nearby.

One of them, Paul Butler, soon joined the family. He married Monet's stepdaughter Suzanne. When she died in 1899, Butler married Marthe, another stepdaughter.

Soon afterward Monet took his art in still another direction. He had always been interested in the effects of light. He began a series in which he would paint the same object in different light conditions. He wanted all the paintings to be exhibited together, so that onlookers could observe how the changes in the light changed the subject. His first series was of haystacks on his property. Another series featured nearby poplar trees.

Monet moved to the village of Giverny in 1883, and it remained his home for the rest of his life. He loved to wander through the farms and pastures that dotted the landscape. *Haystack at Giverny*, which he painted in 1886, reflects this warmth. He would go on to paint a series of pictures featuring haystacks.

One of his most famous series is the facade of Rouen Cathedral. He began the series in 1892 and completed it the following year. There are more than thirty paintings in the series. The effects range from early-morning sunrise, through the noontime sunlight, and then on to sunset and twilight.

Pierre-Auguste Renoir

One of Monet's closest friends, Pierre-Auguste Renoir, was born in the French city of Limoges on February 25, 1841. When he was four, his family moved to Paris. They lived near the Louvre, a famous art museum. Renoir became interested in art during his frequent visits to the Louvre.

As a teenager, he began working in a porcelain factory. Porcelain is a very delicate kind of ceramic that is fired at a high temperature. Renoir painted small scenes on the porcelain and soon acquired a reputation as one of the factory's best artists.

Unfortunately the factory went bankrupt a few years later. Renoir decided that he wanted to remain an artist, so he began studying traditional methods of painting.

Soon afterward he met Monet, Sisley, and Bazille. They wanted to paint in a different style. Often they would paint the same scene standing side by side. Over the next few years, they developed Impressionism. Renoir was especially interested in using Impressionist techniques to show people enjoying themselves. He was part of the first Impressionist exhibition in 1874.

Even so, he could never completely abandon his early training. Starting about 1880, he began painting in a more traditional style, though he continued to use the bright, vivid colors that the Impressionists made popular. Unlike Monet, who rarely showed his subjects' faces in much detail, Renoir's portraits depicted recognizable people.

Renoir was married and had three children. He often depicted his family in his paintings. His son, Jean, became a famous movie director.

In the early 1890s, Renoir developed a severe case of arthritis, a disease that affects the body's joints. It became increasingly painful for him to paint. He may even have had to strap paintbrushes to his wrists. One result was that his brushstrokes became thicker and the outlines of his paintings softer. Despite his discomfort, he continued to work until almost the end of his life. He died on December 3, 1919.

Renoir's *Two Girls at the Piano*

In later life, Monet's flowing white beard made him one of the more recognizable men in France. Posing in his home in Giverny in 1916, Monet appears to be content and happy with his life, but he was suffering from personal and physical problems.

Water Lilies

In 1893 Monet purchased some of the property adjacent to his own so that he could create a water garden. To fill it, he diverted the course of a nearby river. He built several bridges to connect different parts of the garden. The largest of them, a graceful arching structure, appears in many of his paintings from this era.

This garden would become the central motif of his final three decades. "The water garden became a fascinating point of study for Monet," comments art historian K. E. Sullivan. "The reflections of light on the surface of the water, disturbed here and there by the dizzying descent of the dragonflies, the splash of a frog, the movement of an unseen fish became an obsession. The rich expanse of foliage and the deluge of brilliantly colored and beautifully appointed flowers presented an overwhelming riot of perfectly planned wildness, and exotic growth peaks from beneath the surface of the lustrous pond."[1]

Five years later he began what would become an especially noted series. It centered on the abundance of water lilies that grew in the water garden.

By then, his son Jean had married Blanche Hoschedé, making her both Monet's stepdaughter and his daughter-in-law. Blanche was also a painter. She was the only one of Monet's children to follow in his career footsteps.

With his increasing wealth and fame, Monet was able to resume his traveling. By this time several of the children were married. The others

were old enough to take care of themselves. As a result, Alice was able to accompany Monet during his trips.

In 1899, 1900, and 1901, they visited London. Many of Monet's best paintings were born on this trip. Some were painted on the spot. Many others were completed in the studio back in Giverny.

In succeeding years he and Alice made frequent trips in a new car that Monet was able to purchase. The highlight of these motor trips came in 1904 when they drove all the way to Spain. The roads were not good and roadside facilities were very primitive.

In 1908 and 1909 they made railroad trips to Venice, Italy. They had an especially good time there. Monet didn't realize it then, but the second trip would mark the last time he would travel. For the rest of his life, he stayed at Giverny.

Also in 1909, he held an exhibit of forty-eight of the water lilies canvases. The reception was vastly different from the first Impressionist exhibition thirty-five years earlier.

"One has never seen anything like it," declared one reviewer. "These studies of water lilies and still water in every possible effect of light and at every hour of the day are beautiful to a degree which one can hardly express without seeming to exaggerate. . . . There is no other living artist who could have given us these marvelous effects of light and shadow, this glorious feast of color."[2]

Not long before these flattering words were written, Monet came to a grim realization. His eyesight was going bad. For a painter who was dependent on recognizing the subtle changes in light as it fell across an object, this was terrible news. But he continued to work.

Soon afterward tragedy struck. His wife was diagnosed with leukemia, a very serious disease of the blood. Alice died on May 19, 1911. Monet was devastated, probably even more so than when he had lost Camille thirty-two years earlier. This marriage had lasted much longer, and a good portion of it had been accompanied by financial success and increasing fame.

The Water Lily Pond; Pink Harmony. One of Monet's favorite subjects in the 1890s was his water garden. In 1899, he painted ten views of the pond and the bridge that spanned it. The paintings demonstrate the changing effects of light on the same subject.

"I am totally worn out," he wrote a friend. "Time passes and I cannot make anything out of my sad existence. I don't have the taste for anything and don't even have the courage to write."[3] To another friend, he confessed that he was "going to give up painting forever."[4]

While he didn't follow through on this grim prediction, it was especially depressing for him to work in his studio on the canvases he had begun while he and Alice were in Venice. "I should have left them just as they were, as souvenirs of such happy days spent with my dear Alice."[5]

His woes continued. Early in 1914, Jean died after a painful illness. His widow, Blanche, became Monet's primary caregiver and companion. His eyesight grew worse, and he realized that he had cataracts. He wanted to have them removed, but was afraid of possible side effects.

Several months later, World War I broke out. The war seriously depressed Monet and he wasn't able to accomplish much work. One of his close friends was Georges Clemenceau, who became prime minister of France during the war. Clemenceau sometimes visited Monet at his studio, and tried to encourage him to paint. He suggested a large series of water lilies.

With Blanche also encouraging him, in 1916 Monet began what became known as *Grandes Décorations des Nymphéas*. These were massive canvases depicting the water lilies and other scenes from his water garden. They were far larger than anything he had attempted previously. He had to build a new and much larger studio to accommodate them.

Meanwhile his eyesight continued to deteriorate. In 1923 he finally agreed to an operation to remove the cataracts. It was a partial success— he could see much better out of one of his eyes. He worked steadily on the large paintings.

Monet had been a smoker for much of his life. This habit finally caught up with him in 1926. In October he was diagnosed with pulmonary sclerosis, a serious disease of the lungs. By then he had completed *Grandes Décorations des Nymphéas*.

Claude Monet died at home in his beloved Giverny on December 5, 1926. He lived to be eighty-six years old. He had a simple funeral. There were no religious ceremonies because he didn't believe in God.

The following year, the *Grandes Décorations des Nymphéas* was installed in a special permanent exhibition in Paris. It provided a fitting recognition by the French government that Monet was literally a national treasure. The teenager who had begun his art career by drawing caricatures ended it seven decades later as a master who had transformed the world of painting.

World War I in France

When World War I broke out in early August of 1914, the French, the British, and the Russians faced Germany and the empire of Austria-Hungary. The German strategy was to win a quick and decisive victory in the West. Then they would transfer troops to the Russian front, where they also expected a relatively short conflict. When the war began, the Germans launched a massive invasion of France. For several weeks they made rapid progress, but their offensive bogged down in early September.

Both sides began digging trenches. Within a few weeks, the two sides faced each other a few hundred yards apart in a huge double line that stretched from the English Channel across northern France to its ending point at the border of Switzerland. The Swiss were neutral, which means they didn't take sides in the conflict.

The men lived in horrible conditions. The trenches frequently flooded when it rained. They often had to eat cold, unappetizing food. If they stuck their head above the trench, they risked being shot by snipers.

For much of the time the two sides faced each other without moving. Occasionally one side—usually the British and French—would launch an attack. It would begin with a long artillery bombardment. Then the men would swarm out of the trenches. Many would be cut down by machine-gun fire. Even if the attack went well at first, it was rare to gain more than a mile or two of enemy territory. Often even those meager gains would soon be lost.

The stalemate lasted for several years. Millions of men on both sides were killed or badly wounded. The turning point came a little over a year after the United States entered the

A French watchman in World War I

war in April 1917. Enough American troops arrived in France to make a difference. In conjunction with the French and British, they broke through the German trenches. The Germans surrendered on November 11, 1918.

Giverny was within forty miles of the front lines. Sometimes Monet could hear the roar of the artillery. Field hospitals for wounded French soldiers were located nearby. Monet donated most of the vegetables from his garden to the hospitals.

1840	Claude Monet is born on November 14 in Paris, France
1845	Moves to Le Havre
1857	Meets Eugène Boudin
1858	Mother dies
1859	Leaves for Paris and enters Académie Suisse, where he meets Camille Pissarro
1861	Begins military service
1862	Ends military service; begins studying in Paris with Charles Gleyre
1865	Meets Camille Doncieux; two of his paintings are accepted by the official Salon
1866	*Woman in the Green Dress*, with Camille as the model, is accepted by the Salon
1867	His artworks are ejected by the Salon; birth of son Jean
1868	Reportedly tries to commit suicide
1870	Marries Camille Doncieux
1871	Settles in Argenteuil
1874	Is important part of the first Impressionist exhibition
1878	Moves to Vétheuil; birth of son Michel; Hoschedé family joins the Monets
1879	Camille dies
1881	Moves to Poissy with the Hoschedé family
1883	Rents farm at Giverny
1890	Buys farm at Giverny
1892	Marries Alice Hoschedé
1893	Establishes water garden
1898	Begins first series of water lily paintings
1899	Takes first of three successive trips to London
1904	Claude and Alice drive to Spain
1908	Eyesight begins to fail
1911	Alice dies
1914	Son Jean dies
1916	Begins *Grandes Décorations des Nymphéas*, second and much larger series of water lily paintings
1923	Has operation on eyes to remove cataracts
1926	Dies on December 5 in Giverny

1789   George Washington becomes the first U.S. president; the French Revolution begins.

1795   France adopts the metric system of measurement.

1799   French painter Ferdinand Delacroix is born.

1804   Napoléon I becomes French emperor.

1815   Napoléon loses the Battle of Waterloo and is exiled to St. Helena Island in the South Atlantic Ocean.

1836   Texas wins independence from Mexico after being defeated at the Battle of the Alamo.

1837   Victoria becomes queen of England.

1840   William Henry Harrison is elected as the ninth U.S. president; he dies the following April after one month in office.

1845   The U.S. Naval Academy opens at Annapolis, Maryland.

1848   The discovery of gold in California sets off the California gold rush the following year.

1854   Famous French magazine *Le Figaro* begins publication.

1863   Delacroix dies.

1870   The Franco-Prussian War begins; it ends the following year.

1876   Alexander Graham Bell invents the telephone.

1883   Former frontier scout William F. Cody organizes his Wild West Show; sharpshooter Annie Oakley becomes a featured attraction.

1889   Construction of the Eiffel Tower in Paris, France, is completed.

1896   The modern Olympic Games begin in Athens, Greece.

1901   Queen Victoria dies, ending the longest reign in British history.

1906   Spanish artist Pablo Picasso enters his Cubist Period.

1914   World War I begins.

1918   World War I ends.

1925   Calvin Coolidge becomes the thirtieth president of the United States.

1929   The Great Depression begins.

1939   World War II begins.

1945   World War II ends.

1969   U.S. astronauts Neil Armstrong and Buzz Aldrin land on the moon.

1976   The United States of America celebrates the 200th anniversary of its establishment.

1985   *Impression: Sunrise* is stolen from the Musée Marmottan in Paris.

2007   Monet's works continue to be exhibited, such as at the Cleveland Museum of Art.

Chapter I. *Impression: Sunrise* Makes a Big Impression
1. Louis Leroy, *Le Charivari*, "Exhibition of the Impressionists," April 25, 1874. http://www.artchive.com/galleries/1874/74leroy.htm
2. Ibid.
3. Ibid.
4. Emile Cardon, *La Presse*, "The Exhibition of the Revoltes," April 29, 1874. http://artchive.com/galleries/1874/74critic.htm
5. Impressionism, "About Impressionism," http://www.impressionism.org/teachimpress/browse/aboutimpress.htm
6. Jules Castagnary, *Le Siecle*, "L'exposition du boulevard des Capucines-Les impressionnistes," April 29, 1874. http://artchive.com/galleries/1874/74critic.htm
7. Christoph Heinrich, *Monet* (New York: Barnes and Noble Books, 2001), p. 45.

Chapter 2. Early Life
1. Claude Monet, "Claude Monet by Himself," http://www.intermonet.com/biograph/autobigb.htm
2. Ibid.
3. Ibid.
4. William C. Seitz, *Monet* (New York: Harry N. Abrams, 1982), p. 12.
5. Monet.
6. Ibid.
7. Ibid.
8. Seitz, p. 13.
9. Monet.
10. Ibid.
11. Ibid.

12. Trewin Copplestone, *Claude Monet* (New York: Gramercy Books, 1999), p. 14.
13. Lisa MacDonald, "Edouard Manet," http://www.artchive.com/artchive/M/manet.html

Chapter 3. Years of Struggle
1. Trewin Copplestone, *Claude Monet* (New York: Gramercy Books, 1999), p. 15.
2. Christoph Heinrich, *Monet* (New York: Barnes and Noble Books, 2001), p. 23.
3. Ibid., p. 46.
4. Paul Hayes Tucker, *Claude Monet: Life and Art* (New Haven, Connecticut: Yale University Press, 1995), p. 57.
5. Haussmann and New Paris, http://www.mtholyoke.edu/courses/rschwart/hist255-s01/mapping-paris/Haussmann.html

Chapter 4. Giverny
1. Christoph Heinrich, *Monet* (New York: Barnes and Noble Books, 2001), pp. 71-72.

Chapter 5. Water Lilies
1. K. E. Sullivan, *Monet* (London: Flame Tree Publishing, 1996), p. 69.
2. Paul Hayes Tucker, *Claude Monet: Life and Art* (New Haven, Connecticut: Yale University Press, 1995), p. 196.
3. Ibid., p. 200.
4. Ibid.
5. Ibid.

For Young Adults

Björk, Christina. *Linnea in Monet's Garden*. Translated by Joan Sandin. New York: R & S Books, 1987.

Hodge, Susie. *Claude Monet*. New York: Franklin Watts, 2002.

Muhlberger, Richard. *What Makes a Monet a Monet?* New York: Viking Juvenile, 2002.

Waldron, Ann. *First Impressions: Claude Monet*. New York: Harry N. Abrams, 1991.

Welton, Jude. *Monet*. New York: Dorling Kindersley, 2000.

Works Consulted

Copplestone, Trewin. *Claude Monet*. New York: Gramercy Books, 1999.

Forge, Andrew. *Claude Monet in the Art Institute of Chicago*. Chicago: Art Institute of Chicago, 1995.

Heinrich, Christoph. *Monet*. New York: Barnes and Noble Books, 2001.

Holmes, Caroline. *Monet at Giverny*. London: Cassell & Company, 2001.

Joel, David. *Monet at Vétheuil 1878-1883*. Woodbridge, England: Antique Collectors Club Ltd., 2007.

Potts, Vanessa. *Essential Monet*. Bath, England: Parragon Publishing, 2002.

Seitz, William C. *Monet*. New York: Harry N. Abrams, 1982.

Sullivan, K. E. Monet. London: Flame Tree Publishing, 1996.

Tucker, Paul Hayes. *Claude Monet: Life and Art*. New Haven, Connecticut: Yale University Press, 1995.

On the Internet

Giverny and Vernon: In the Heart of Impressionism: *Biography of Claude Monet*
http://giverny.org/monet/biograph/

Claude Monet Life and Art: "Claude Monet by Himself: My History"
http://www.intermonet.com/biograph/autobigb.htm

Nancy Doyle Fine Art: *Artist Profile: Claude Monet*
http://www.ndoylefineart.com/monet.html

The Impressionist Movement and Its Greatest Painters: *Impressionism: Biography of Claude Monet*
http://www.impressionniste.net/monet_claude.htm

Claude Monet (1840-1926): *Biography*
http://www.expo-monet.com/2.cfm

ibiblio: *WebMuseum, Paris*, "Monet, Claude: *Madame Gaudibert*"
http://www.ibiblio.org/wm/paint/auth/monet/early/gaudibert/

Impressionism: *About Impressionism*
http://www.impressionism.org/teachimpress/browse/aboutimpress.htm

Stern, Jean. "The Development of Southern California Impressionism"
http://www.tfaoi.com/aa/2aa/2aa643.htm

Artchive: *First Impressionist Exhibition: Contemporary Criticism*
http://artchive.com/galleries/1874/74critic.htm

Artchive: "Nicolas Poussin (1594–1665)"
http://www.artchive.com/artchive/P/poussin.html

MacDonald, Lisa. "Edouard Manet (1832-1883)"
http://www.artchive.com/artchive/M/manet.html

France Monthly: *Paris, City of Light*
http://www.francemonthly.com/n/1001/index.php

France in the Age of Les Misérables: *Haussmann and New Paris*
http://www.mtholyoke.edu/courses/rschwart/hist255-s01/mapping-paris/Haussmann.html

Artelino Art Auctions: *Biography of Auguste Renoir—1841–1919*
http://www.artelino.com/articles/auguste_renoir.asp

art critic
A person who knows a great deal about art and makes judgments about the value of particular works based on his or her knowledge.

bourgeoisie (bourzh-wah-ZEE)
Members of the middle class of a country.

cataracts (KAA-tuh-raks)
Cloudy covering of the eyes that prevents the normal amount of light from entering.

contemporary (kun-TEM-puh-rayr-ee)
Happening at the same time; happening during one's lifetime.

dilapidated (duh-LAH-puh-day-tid)
In very bad condition; nearly ready to fall apart.

dowry (DOW-ree)
Money or something else of value that the family of a bride gives to the groom at the time of the wedding.

embryonic (em-bree-AH-nik)
In an early stage of development.

initiates (ih-NIH-shee-uts)
Persons who have special knowledge in a certain field.

landscape (LAND-skayp)
A painting or drawing that primarily depicts the artist's surroundings, though it may also include figures of people.

portraits (POR-truts)
Artwork that primarily depicts a person or persons.

seascape (SEE-skayp)
A painting or drawing that depicts a scene at the ocean.

sou (SOO)
A French coin having little value.

still life
A painting of inanimate objects.